A History of
The Romani People

A History of
The Romani People

HRISTO KYUCHUKOV • IAN HANCOCK

BOYDS MILLS PRESS

To my son Roberto with love
"Murre čikne chaveske Robertoske bute kamimasa"

—H. K.

To my children, my treasure, Malik and Chloë
"Murre čhavorrenge, m'o mandjin, o Malik thaj e Xloje"

—I. H.

Text copyright © 2005 by Hristo Kyuchukov and Ian Hancock
All rights reserved

Boyds Mills Press, Inc.
A Highlights Company
815 Church Street
Honesdale, Pennsylvania 18431
Printed in China

Publisher Cataloging-in-Publication Data (U.S.)

Kyuchukov, Hristo.
A history of the Romani people / Hristo Kyuchukov ; Ian Hancock.
[   ] p. : col. photos.. ;   cm.
ISBN 1-56397-962-4
1. Romanies — History. 2. Romanies — Social life and customs. I. Hancock, Ian.
II . Title.
909/.0491497 22   DX155.R66K98   2005

First edition, 2005
The text of this book is set in 12-point Berkeley.

Visit our Web site at www.boydsmillspress.com

10 9 8 7 6 5 4 3 2 1

Hristo Kyuchukov as a child with his parents.

"I want people to know what being a Romani is like."

I was a young teacher in a small village in Bulgaria teaching Muslim Romani children when the Communists forced all of us to give up our Muslim names and adopt Orthodox Christian ones. I saw pain and tears in the eyes of the children; but it was too dangerous not to obey. We were all frightened. For twenty-two years my name had been Hussein, but in just three days I was renamed Hristo. Many years later I became a university professor, and I always tell my students the story of what happened. That is why this book was written. I want people to know what being a Romani is like.

A group photo from Ian Hancock's family album.

"The Romani people are a real people."

I grew up outside London in a Romani family just one generation away from wagon life. Even as a child I would join my relatives who went hop picking in the south of England. Although I didn't finish high school, through an unusual set of circumstances I went on to become a United Nations ambassador for Romanies, a U.S. Presidential appointee to the Holocaust Council, and a professor at the University of Texas at Austin, where I am now Director of the Romani Archives and Documentation Center.

Origins

A young girl from a nomadic family at the Puskar Fair in India.

Using language and cultural clues, historians have shown that Gypsies are originally from northern India. When Muslim soldiers attacked parts of northwestern India one thousand years ago, groups of Hindus with similar languages came together to resist the invaders, forming a warrior caste called *Rajput*.

When those Rajputs and their camp followers were defeated, they were incorporated into their captors' armies and brought westward into Anatolia, where their presence was first noted in the eleventh century. By the late thirteenth century, Islamic expansion had again displaced them, this time up into the Balkan regions of Europe. The name *Romani* may have developed from those living in the Kingdom of Rum, part of where present-day Turkey is. After a couple of hundred years, they began to migrate again, this time toward Europe.

As they moved, these travelers adopted cultural and religious ideas from the different peoples around them, combining these new beliefs with their old ones.

◀ Contemporary Indians travel much like those who left the country one thousand years ago.

▼ The Rajput groups had to navigate high mountain passes when they left India.

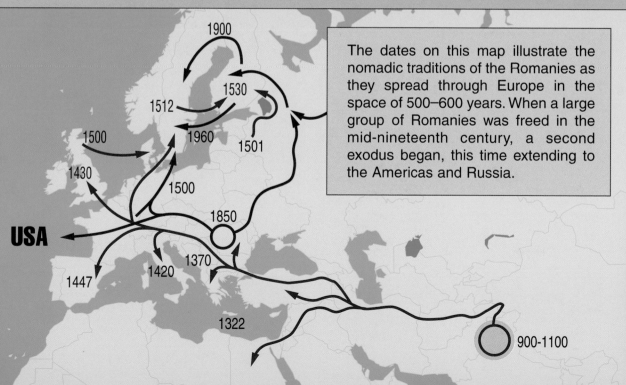

The dates on this map illustrate the nomadic traditions of the Romanies as they spread through Europe in the space of 500–600 years. When a large group of Romanies was freed in the mid-nineteenth century, a second exodus began, this time extending to the Americas and Russia.

1900

1530

1512

1500

1960

1501

1430

1500

USA

1850

1447

1420

1370

1322

900-1100

Names of Romanies

Although there are many different names for a Romani, the most common one is Gypsy, born from a fifteenth-century belief in Europe that the dark skin and unfamiliar, colorful clothing of these travelers marked them as Egyptians. Romanies are also called Tsigani, Zigeurner, Zingari, and Gitanos (from the Greek word *Atsiganos*, which means "untouchable"). These names have a negative connotation, and Romanies do not like them. We prefer to be called Romanies, as we call ourselves. Although Romani people have learned to use the official languages of the countries in which they live, their own language remains essential to them. Through the years, the Romani people have enriched their original language, which was mainly Indian, with words from the Greek, Armenian, Romanian, Turkish, and Slavic languages.

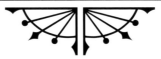

▲ A group of Polish musicians entertains on a street corner in hopes of earning some money.

THE ROMANI LANGUAGE

The base of Romani and all its dialects is Sanskrit. Rajput and their followers spoke a variety of languages that had evolved from Sanskrit when they were forced to leave India around the year 1000. As the immigrants spread out, they added new words from the countries where they lived, words describing all the new things they saw and learned.

Until about one hundred years ago, we Romanies passed along our stories, history, and music by word of mouth alone. Recently, scholars (like the authors of this book) have been writing everything down so that both Romanies and non-Romani people can understand the Romani way of life. Although there are now more than sixty dialects, current Romanies most often use Vlax in the classroom and for conferences. This language is spoken by more than half of all Romanies. It is derived from the Romani descendants of slaves in Romania.

▲ These three generations of Romanies near Bilbao, Spain, do not speak much Romani since Spain was one of the countries to prohibit its use.

English	Vlax	Pronunciation
Thank you!	*Najis tuke!*	**NAH**-YEES **TOO**-KEH
You're welcome!	*Naj pala soste!*	**NY** POLLA **SOSS**-TAY
Good-bye	*Dža Devlesa!*	**ZHAH** DEV-**LESS**-SA
What is your name?	*Sar bučhos?*	**SAR** BOO-**SHOSS**
Where are you from?	*Katar aves?*	**KAT**-TAR AH-**VESS**
Where do you live?	*Kaj bešes?*	**KY** BESH-**ESS**
Can I help you?	*Šaj žutiv tut?*	**SHY** ZHOO-**TEEV TOO**T
Let's go together.	*Kethanes džastar.*	KET-AH-**NESS ZHASS**-TAR
How? Why?	*Sar? Anda soste?*	**SAR** ONDA **SOSS**-TAY
Where? When?	*Kaj? Kana?*	**KY KONNA**
Here; There	*Kathe; Kothe*	KAH-**TAY** KOH-**TAY**
Yes; No	*Va; Na*	**VAH NAH**

Traditions and Religion

▲ This Romani woman is leaving favorite items for the deceased that might be used in the afterlife.

For centuries we Romanies have traveled from town to town and country to country, speaking our own language and zealously maintaining our own customs and time-honored rituals. Although we have been enslaved, murdered, persecuted, and discriminated against for a thousand years, we have managed to keep our identity and have never abandoned our way of life.

In addition to the Indian language, a number of Romani traditions originally came from India. Music, weddings, funerals, and family habits still have clear similarities with Indian practices and Hindu religious beliefs. These Romani beliefs are central to who we are, but we have also often adopted the religion worshiped in the areas where we live. This is the reason why Orthodox Christian, Muslim, Roman Catholic, and Pentecostal customs can be found in different Romani communities.

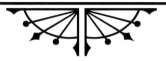

◀ Travellers in Ireland set up camp in a churchyard in County Galway just before a popular horse fair.

▼ Our people are proud of our expertise with horses, and for hundreds of years the buying, selling, and trading of horses has had great economic importance.

Engagement and Marriage

Families, with all their numerous relations, form the basic unit of Romani life. Everything revolves around the family, and all the events and celebrations of family life become significant.

Engagements and marriages are especially important because they continue the family's survival. All Romanies are expected to marry, and both boys and girls are expected to marry someone within their community.

In many families, the parents rather than the young people arrange the marriage. Marriages often consolidate family businesses, and the groom's family pays a dowry to the bride's family to compensate for their loss of a money earner. From the wedding day on, the bride formally joins the groom's family.

Romani weddings are joyful three-day events, combining both European and Indian traditions. On the first day, the bride's close female friends and relatives help her bathe and braid her hair in preparation for the wedding.

On the second day, the groom and his relatives bring gifts to the bride and her family. The two families dine together to formally confirm the marriage.

On the third day, there is a public celebration with many friends and family members, usually all Romanies. The groom's family comes to the bride's house to take her to the festivities. Then there is a big party with music, dancing, and tables full of good food. A hollowed-out loaf of bread is passed around so that guests may put in gifts of money.

▲ Modern Romani weddings combine old
and new customs.

◀ Enthusiastic dancing is typical of Romani
weddings and celebrations.

The Arrival of a Baby

▲ Young people get an early start in adult chores. This girl is responsible for the chickens.

A baby's birth is special, just as it is in every culture. Romani women tend to the mother-to-be and help with the birth, which is usually at home. After the birth, there are special ceremonies to introduce the baby to his or her father.

After two weeks, the baby is baptized. The baby is given two names. The first is the Romani name by which the baby is called within the family and by other Romanies. The second is for use in the non-Roma world.

Children

Children are welcomed by everyone in the family group. They become everyone's responsibility. They learn skills by watching and imitating the grown-ups. Of course, they also go to school. But as important as schools are, for Romani children they can be uncomfortable and even dangerous places. Our children often don't yet read and write a second language at grade level. School food is unfamiliar and not cooked by a Romani. Textbooks say negative things about other Romanies. Finally, if children make non-Romani friends, these new friends may interfere with traditional values and customs.

Three typical scenes of travellers' children show an outdoor cooking setup, a pitched tent, and a boy with his pup.

15

Wagons

For years Romanies had to move from place to place in order to make a living. Because of this way of life, we lived for hundreds of years in horse-drawn wagons and carts. Although most Romanies have given up the traveling life these days, some continue to travel from town to town in motorized trailers. They still have everything they need inside: beds, tables and chairs, wash basins, cooking equipment, toys, and clothes.

Shapes of traveling wagons vary around the world, from Scandinavia to Turkey, but they are all home.

▶ Think about how important well-made wagon wheels must be. Good wheels are almost as valuable as a good horse.

▼ In some parts of the world, Romanies make camp together in order to enjoy each others' company and share meals.

Occupations

▲ A Romani woodworker roughing out a bowl near the forest of Balteni, in Romania.

Romanies have had to be flexible and resourceful to earn a living while on the road. Different families have specialized in certain professions for generations, such as horse trading, blacksmithing, metalworking, furniture making, playing traditional music, and fortune-telling. Romanies are thought to have brought their expert metalworking skills from Asia, along with their musical talent for playing the violin and drums. Using horses as they migrated, Romanies became knowledgeable about the healing and training of these animals and others as well. Throughout Europe the Romanies would entertain in towns and villages with trained bears.

Ever since they arrived in Europe, Romanies have been famous as fortune-tellers, and many outsiders associate fortune-telling specifically with them. Using experience and intuition, these Romani women read palms and tea leaves, see visions in crystal balls, analyze the future from reading cards, and interpret the significance of numbers.

▲ A fortune-teller sees clues to the future as she lays out her special deck of cards for a customer.

◄ Romanies are well known as blacksmiths, as well as for the excellent care we give our horses.

19

▲ Spanish flamenco dancing is closely related to traditional Romani dancing.

Romani songs and musicians have been popular for centuries all over Europe. Composers Haydn, Brahms, and Liszt, for instance, used Romani melodies in their classical compositions. Bizet's well-known opera *Carmen* is the story of a beautiful and reckless Spanish Gypsy girl. More recently, some of us have become well known as influential jazz musicians, like guitarist Django Reinhardt.

The great tradition of Russian choral singing began in the late eighteenth century when Count Orlov created a male chorus using his own slaves (known in Russia as serfs), many of whom were Romanies. The traveling chorus was so successful and popular that the count freed his singers ten years later.

Romanies are recognized as professionals in many occupations. Athletic Romanies are often boxers. Rita Hayworth and Charlie Chaplin were popular movie stars. Former president of the United States William Clinton has Romani ancestors.

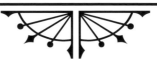

▶ For years Romanies led trained dancing bears through the streets of small and large towns all over Europe. This is becoming rare because many people believe that this practice is unfair to the bears.

▼ Refining his banjo skills on a summer day, this man continues a long tradition of Romani music.

Traditional Law

▲ The coronation of Romani "King" Janusz Kwiek in Warsaw, Poland, 1937. The Kwiek family attempted to unify the Romanies by establishing a dynasty and winning non-Romani (*gadjo*) support in favor of a Romani homeland. Despite promises, no homeland was established. Instead, many Romanies were rounded up and killed.

The Romani legal system provides a structure that protects Romani society. Romani law is self-defined, and it is wholly independent of any country's formal legal system. There are variations among Romanies, but more than half, the Vlax speakers in particular, use these practices.

Every family group is ruled by a wise older member who resolves day-to-day problems in the community. Larger problems are referred to a Romani court called a *Kris*. A Kris meets only occasionally and includes a panel of judges made up of Romanies from other groups. There are no lawyers; each side testifies for itself, backed up (often loudly) by other family members and witnesses.

If a defendant is found guilty, he or she can be punished by fines or by temporary or permanent banishment from the community. There are no Romani jails. For a Romani, complete exile from the community is the worst fate imaginable.

Through the years, several of the larger groups of Romanies have designated important and influential men as *bare* (leaders). These men have power within their group, but this is not a hereditary position. Therefore, it is not necessarily passed down from father to son.

WHEN A ROMANI DIES

Romani groups follow a variety of traditions when a family member dies. During this time the spirit world must be kept away from the family, and the dying person is often moved out of the home to a nearby shelter set up for just this purpose. After death the whole family participates in mourning rituals until the burial. Personal items of the dead person are given away or put into the grave. Romani people believe relatives can communicate with them even after death. Advice may be sought from departed relatives and friends, and family members look for signs that the dead person has sent a solution to a problem they face.

◀ Burning the possessions and wagon of a Romani who died in twentieth-century Great Britain carries on a practice brought from India hundreds of years ago.

▼ This contemporary Romani from the United States keeps her deceased relative company by sharing her coffee.

Hardships

When the Romanies in Romania were finally freed in 1864, the poet Adriano Colocci wrote a poem celebrating their freedom. A favorite verse is:

Come running, beloved brothers all—
Today, come running all;
For freed we are, by the Rumanian
  prince.
Let us cry out with full voice,
So let it be!

Throughout our history, we Romani have endured many hardships. Because we looked and acted differently, because we kept to ourselves, and because we were not allowed to stay in one place long enough to become part of a community, we made other people suspicious. Rumors were whispered about us, and people began to hate and fear "the Gypsies."

To calm these fears, governments passed laws to restrict the movements and lives of Romanies. Some laws said Romanies could not go where they wanted. Other laws took away their right to speak their own language, to raise their own children, to wear traditional clothing, and to play Romani music.

During the Roman Catholic Inquisition in fifteenth-century Spain, thousands of Romanies were arrested. Some were killed, and a few were given to Christopher Columbus when he crossed the Atlantic Ocean. Other countries deported Romanies to their colonies. Claiming that Gypsies were born criminals, Portugal sent Romanies to Brazil, and England shipped them off first to North America and then to Australia.

▲ For hundreds of years, Romanies have camped just outside the walls of castles, towns, and villages, forbidden to enter.

◄ A married couple from the mid-nineteenth century. The gold coins on their clothing, represent much of the family wealth.

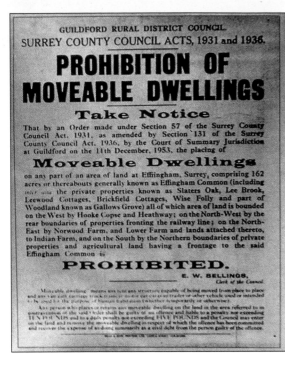

For five hundred years in Romania, the Romani people were legally slaves. But even the abolition of slavery in 1864 did not mean liberty for Romanies. As the Industrial Revolution forced farm workers off the land and into the backbreaking routines of factory life, Romanies set themselves apart by continuing to travel. Soon Romanies were expelled from many areas because they had no proof of steady jobs or permanent homes.

During World War II, the Nazi government in Germany, in their quest for a pure Aryan race, targeted Romanies for persecution. More than one million Romanies were sent to concentration camps and murdered in the Holocaust, which destroyed many of Europe's Jews and other minorities.

▲ One of hundreds of posted notices reminding the Romanies to keep moving. This one is from England.

▶ Romanies were kept on the move all over Europe, especially during World War II. This group is winding through a town in 1943.

◄ In the 1920s, even before Hitler came to power, Romanies in Germany were being rounded up and imprisoned.

◄ Life in the Belvez concentration camp in World War II. Romanies were kept separate from other prisoners when they were arrested. In prison they had to take care of themselves, but they had only the clothing, bedding, and tools they came with, and they were given little food. Most died or were killed before the war ended in 1945.

Life Today

▲ On his way to a horse fair, a Romani weaves his way through tangled traffic.

▼ A French postage stamp honoring jazz musician Django Reinhardt.

Even today, in many countries Romanies still face discrimination. In some places we are forced to live with curfews in walled ghettos with no running water or electricity. Although most Romanies now live in houses, we are often attacked, and our homes are set on fire by the same kinds of people who have always felt threatened by anyone different.

Romanies have had a hard time developing organizations to unite our different groups, but this cooperation is vital. Thoughtful Romanies have known for years that discrimination will not change unless everyone else begins to understand us and our way of life. There are now organizations that work to promote the Romani language, civil rights, and cross-cultural acceptance.

Modern Romanies try to keep their language and traditions alive while living in cities and villages all over the world. There are more than twelve million Romanies, and in Europe we are by far the largest minority group. We go to school and college, and work in a wide variety of professions, as teachers, lawyers, doctors, engineers, and journalists, as well as in traditional occupations.

It is remarkable that we Romanies survive, despite persecution, being one thousand years from our homeland, with no country to call our own. Through the years we have learned to adapt to every continent on earth, still keeping our families, language, and culture intact.

▲ A group of young Romani children.

◀ This contemporary family has recently given up their caravan and settled into the English countryside.

ROMANI POPULATION AROUND THE WORLD

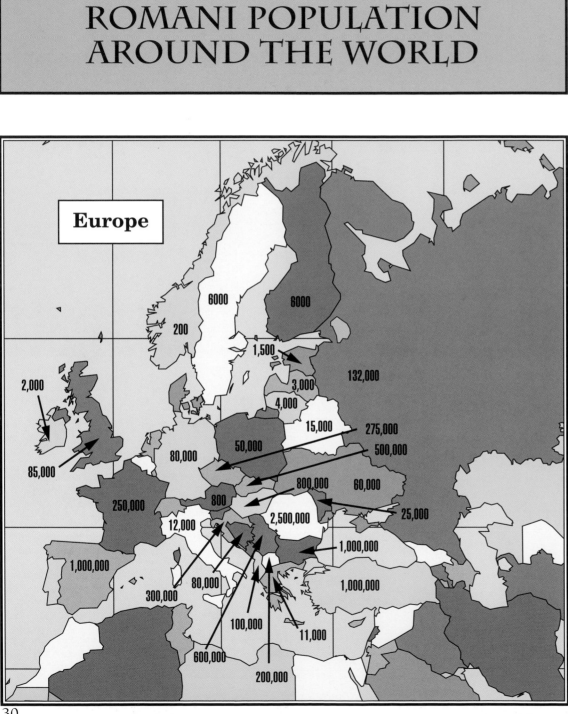

Europe

6000
6000
200
1,500
132,000
3,000
4,000
2,000
15,000
275,000
80,000
50,000
500,000
85,000
800,000
60,000
250,000
800
2,500,000
25,000
12,000
1,000,000
1,000,000
1,000,000
80,000
300,000
100,000
11,000
600,000
200,000

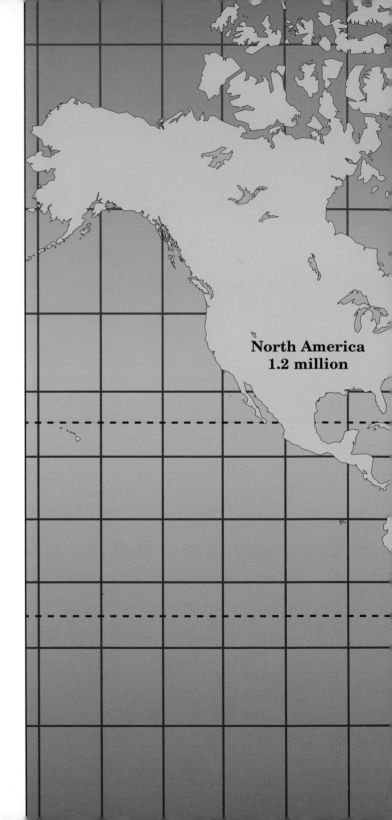

**North America
1.2 million**

Europe
9 million

Asia
100,000

Africa
50,000

ntral
nd
America
illion

Australia
and New Zealand
12,000

31

INDEX

PHOTO CREDITS

Photographs courtesy of Ian Hancock, with the following exceptions:

Bruce Dale/National Geographic Image Collection: 25 (right), 28 (top), 10

Shirdi Maherashtra/Dinodia Picture Agency: 7 (top left)

© Doranne Jacobson: 6, 9

John Elk III/Bruce Coleman Inc.: 7 (bottom right)

Hristo Kyuchukov: 5 (top)

Mathias Oppersdorff: 11 (left), 15 (all), 21 (left)

Ivan Melnyk/Bruce Coleman Inc.: jacket background

Ginger Myers: 23 (right), 29 (right)

Helen Wellstead: 29 (left)